FERRETS

FERRETS

A Carolrhoda Nature Watch Book

by Sylvia A. Johnson

Carolrhoda Books, Inc. / Minneapolis

The author would like to thank Sally Heber, president of the American Ferret Association, for her advice and assistance. Thanks also to the members of the Minnesota chapter of the AFA for sharing their favorite ferret stories.

Carolrhoda Books, Inc., c/o The Lerner Publishing Group
241 First Avenue North, Minneapolis, MN 55401

Website address: www.lernerbooks.com

LIBRARY OF CONGRESS CATALOGING-IN-PUBLICATION DATA

Johnson, Sylvia A.
  Ferrets / by Sylvia A. Johnson.
     p.   cm.
  "A Carolrhoda nature watch book."
  Includes index.
  Summary: Presents information about the physical characteristics, behavior, and history of ferrets and discusses keeping and caring for these animals as pets.
  ISBN 1-57505-014-5
  1. Ferrets as pets — Juvenile literature. 2. Ferret — Juvenile literature. [1. Ferret. 2. Ferrets as pets. 3. Pets.]
  I. Title.
SF429.F47J64 1997
636'.974447—dc20   96–7068

Photographs are reproduced through the courtesy of:
© Ron Kimball, front cover, p. 24 (left); © Beth Davidow, back cover, pp. 19, 20 (top), 21, 24 (right), 31 (both), 32, 35, 36, 38, 45 (bottom); Nancy Smedstad, IPS, pp. 4, 6, 17, 20 (bottom), 22, 23, 29; William H. Allen, Jr., p. 7; © C. Postmus/Root Resources, p. 8 (top); © Susan Alworth, p. 8 (bottom); © Wendy Shattil/Bob Rozinski, pp. 9 (bottom), 12 (bottom), 40; © Alan G. Nelson/Root Resources, p. 9 (right); © Alan & Sandy Carey, pp. 10, 13, 43, 45 (top); © Mary & Lloyd McCarthy/Root Resources, p. 11; © Mike Lane/Aquila Photographics, p. 12 (top); UPI/Corbis-Bettman, p. 14; Sherm Spoelstra, p. 15; Independent Picture Service, p. 16; Barbara DeCorso/AFA, Inc., pp. 18, 26; © Shirley Haley/Top Shots, pp. 25, 27, 30; Traci Stewart, pp. 28, 34, 39 (both); Jennifer Lohman, p. 33; © S. Downer/Aquila Photographics, p. 37; © Mary A. Root/Root Resources, p. 41; © Kenneth W. Fink/Root Resources, p. 42; William Muñoz, p. 44.

CONTENTS

INTRODUCTION

Glancing through an article in the local newspaper, you might come across a sentence like this: "The mayor said that he was going to ferret out the causes of increased crime in the city." *Ferret out* is a common expression. It means "to hunt" or "to search for." But where did this expression come from?

When people ferret something out, they are imitating the behavior of an animal that has lived closely with humans for thousands of years. The expression used in the newspaper article comes from the name of this unique little animal, the domesticated ferret.

Centuries ago, people used tame ferrets to drive rabbits and rodents out of hiding places. In the modern world, the bright-eyed, furry creatures usually don't work for a living. Instead, they are kept as cherished pets by families everywhere.

Top: *The long-tailed weasel is one of the most common North American weasels.* Bottom: *The wolverine is a small but powerful mustelid.*

THE FERRET'S FAMILY TREE

You may never have seen a pet ferret in someone's home, but you are probably familiar with a few of the ferret's wild relatives. Ferrets are not related to rats and mice, as people often think. Instead, their closest cousins in the animal world are weasels, minks, otters, badgers, and skunks. All these animals belong to a scientific family called Mustelidae. Other less familiar **mustelids** include wolverines, martens, polecats, and the rare black-footed ferret.

At first glance, the different wild mustelids don't seem to have very much in common. Some are large animals, like the giant otter of South America, which can weigh more than 60 pounds (27 kg). The giant otter is about 1,000 times bigger than the smallest of the mustelids, the North American least weasel. This tiny animal weighs in at only 1 to 2 ounces (28–56 g).

Mustelids live in many different parts of the world and in very different kinds of environments. Otters large and small are found in both North and South America as well as in Europe, Asia, and Africa. They are expert swimmers and divers, living in freshwater rivers and streams and in the ocean. The martens of North America, Europe, and Asia spend much of their time climbing among the branches of trees. In Africa, Europe, Asia, and North America, badgers dig complicated underground burrows with their long claws.

Two very different types of mustelid: a river otter (below) *and a badger at its burrow* (right)

A black-footed ferret

The black-footed ferret, the rarest of the mustelids, makes its home in prairie-dog burrows on the North American plains. Once thought to be extinct, this wild ferret was rediscovered in Wyoming during the early 1980s. Now black-footed ferrets are being raised in captivity and returned to their home on the plains. (Look for more details of this mustelid success story later in the book.)

Despite their differences, members of the family Mustelidae have many common characteristics. All are **carnivores,** meat-eaters that hunt for their food. All have sharp teeth and claws. Many mustelids, including domesticated ferrets, have a similar physical build, with short, stubby legs and long, often slender bodies. These slim bodies are usually covered with thick, beautiful fur, a feature that has attracted the attention of humans. Mustelids are often trapped for their fur. Some, like the mink, are raised on farms, their fur used to make coats for people.

Perhaps the most famous feature of the mustelids is the ability to produce a strong, unpleasant odor. All mustelids have **scent glands** on various parts of their bodies, including two **anal glands** on their rear ends. These scent glands produce a musky-smelling fluid, which can be used as a means of communication. Minks, otters, polecats, and other mustelids deposit the fluid on objects and on their own bodies to send messages to others of their species.

Mustelids also defend themselves against attackers by discharging or spraying this smelly fluid out of their anal glands. Skunks are the experts in this method of self-defense. They can spray accurately over a distance of six feet. Some polecats also spray in self-defense, but other mustelids simply release the bad-smelling fluid from their anal glands when they are threatened.

Skunks are well known for using a smelly fluid in self-defense, but other mustelids also have this ability.

The European polecat (top) *is probably the ancestor of the domesticated ferret, although the steppe polecat* (bottom) *is also a possible candidate.*

THE DOMESTICATED FERRET

The domesticated ferret is clearly a member of the family Mustelidae. It has the same long, slim body and furry coat as most mustelids. It also has the same lively, curious nature. But scientists are not sure exactly how this tame animal is related to its wild relatives.

One possible ancestor of the domesticated ferret is the steppe polecat of Asia, a mustelid whose scientific name is *Mustela eversmanni.* But most scientists believe that the ferret is probably descended from the European polecat, *Mustela putorius.* In fact, the ferret's scientific name, *Mustela putorius furo,* is based on this connection. Domesticated ferrets look a lot like European polecats, and they have exactly the same number of **chromosomes** (the individual units of genetic material contained in the body's cells). The two kinds of mustelids are able to mate and produce young, which is another sign of a close relationship.

Despite the similarity in their names, the black-footed ferret of North America *(Mustela nigripes)* does not seem to be very closely related to the domesticated ferret. The bodies of the two animals are somewhat different in build (the black-footed ferret is more slender, with larger ears). Their fur also differs in texture and markings. These two members of the mustelid family probably had a common ancestor millions of years ago but now are only distant cousins.

Just like cats and dogs, modern pet ferrets are domesticated animals developed by humans. Early people bred ferrets from wild polecats that they had captured and tamed. Exactly when and where this happened is not known. Many researchers believe that ferrets were domesticated in Europe or Asia at least 500 years before cats were tamed around 2000 B.C.

The black-footed ferret is slimmer than its cousin the domesticated ferret.

A ferret in harness hunts for rabbits in the rubble of a building that was destroyed in Berlin, Germany, during World War II.

In ancient Egypt, people kept tame ferrets as pets and rodent hunters. The Greeks and Romans also used ferrets to get rid of rats and mice and to catch rabbits. The ferret's wild ancestors were rabbit hunters, and domesticated ferrets still had the instinct to pursue this quick-moving prey. Rabbit hunting eventually became one of their most important jobs in the human world.

In Europe during the Middle Ages, many people caught rabbits with the help of tame ferrets. The rich went **ferreting** for sport, while poor people wanted to obtain some rabbit meat for their cooking pots. Released into underground burrows, the ferrets hunted out the rabbits and chased them along the narrow tunnels until they were driven out through escape holes. There the human hunters were waiting to catch and kill the prey. People often placed nets over the holes to trap the rabbits as they emerged.

Domesticated ferrets were probably brought to North America sometime during the early 1700s, and they came to work. As in ancient times, their most important job was rodent control. Sailors often used ferrets to catch the mice and rats that scurried through the holds of sailing ships.

Rodents were also a problem on farms and in other places where crops and grains were stored. To get rid of these pests, a farmer would hire a "ferretmeister," a man who owned dozens of tame ferrets. The ferretmeister brought his ferrets to the farm in cages and released them in the barn or granary. Then the little animals hunted out the rats and mice and drove them from their hiding places. As the rodents fled, people killed them with sticks and shovels.

Ferrets have never lost their instinct for hunting mice.

When modern pesticides were developed in the 1900s, ferrets were no longer needed for rodent control. But there were still some jobs that they could do for people. With their long, slim bodies, ferrets could easily pass through narrow pipes and tubes. So they were sometimes used to carry wires and lines in industry—for example, in manufacturing airplanes—and in construction. Workers attached the wires to collars and used bells or whistles to encourage the ferrets to move through narrow openings.

In Great Britain people still use domesticated ferrets to hunt rabbits. Ferreting hasn't changed much over the centuries, but a few modern touches have been added. Some ferreters put collars with radio transmitters on their animals. By following the transmitter signal, the hunter can track a ferret as it moves through the maze of underground tunnels.

Humans have found yet another use

A hunter in England prepares to use ferrets to flush out rabbits.

for domesticated ferrets: as test animals in medical laboratories. Because ferrets catch the same kinds of colds as people do, they can be used to test new cold medicines and treatments. In the lab as in so many other areas, domesticated ferrets have close connections with the world of humans.

Ferrets have become such popular pets that some owners and breeders exhibit them at ferret shows.

FERRETS AS PETS

In the past, most ferrets worked for a living. The animals stayed in outdoor cages rather than inside people's houses, and they were often treated very harshly. But some ferrets had close relationships with their human masters. Just like domestic cats, they were considered both working animals and valued pets.

According to legend, Queen Elizabeth I of England kept pet **albino** ferrets, with pure-white coats, red eyes, and pink noses. A later English ruler, Queen Victoria, may also have been a ferret owner. In the 1990s, many ordinary people keep domesticated ferrets in their homes.

In the United States alone, there are an estimated 12 million pet ferrets. In fact, the ferret is fast becoming the third most popular pet animal. (Cats are the most popular, and dogs a close second.) What kind of pets do ferrets make? How do they compare to cats and dogs? What is it like to live with these active little animals?

Do Ferrets Make Good Pets?

Most people who own ferrets seem to love them. They can't say enough about what great pets they make. According to these people, ferrets are easier to take care of than dogs. They are small animals that can be kept in the house all the time. They don't need to go for walks, and they can learn to use a litter box, just as cats do.

But ferret admirers claim that ferrets are much more fun to live with than cats. They are more affectionate, more active, and more playful than any feline. And they keep these traits all of their lives, even when they are old.

Pet ferrets require a lot of attention and care.

Doesn't anyone have anything bad to say about ferrets? Well yes, they do. Even the biggest ferret fans admit that ferrets may not be ideal pets for every family since they need quite a bit of attention and care. There are even people who think that ferrets shouldn't be kept as pets at all. The Humane Society of the United States is one organization that holds this view. In a few U. S. states and communities, it is actually illegal to keep pet ferrets. What is behind this controversy over ferrets?

People who are opposed to ferrets as pets claim that they are more like wild animals than domesticated ones. Because of their "wild" nature, these people say, pet ferrets might bite small children without warning, causing serious injuries. Anti-ferret people also worry that ferrets may be carriers of rabies, as many small wild animals are. Another concern is the possibility that pet ferrets might escape and set up colonies in the wild. Groups of wild ferrets might attack and kill wildlife and farm animals.

Two domesticated ferrets enjoy a visit to the outdoors. Both are pets and would be unlikely to survive if left outdoors permanently.

Those who think that ferrets make good pets have answers to all these objections. These people point out that ferrets have been domesticated for thousands of years and have lost many of their wild habits. An escaped ferret would be very unlikely to survive in the wild. It would not be able to find food and would probably be killed by other animals. Surveys have supported these claims: there is no evidence that domesticated ferrets are living in the wild anywhere in the United States.

Ferret defenders don't deny that pet ferrets may nip or bite their owners, especially when they are young. Kittens and puppies do the same thing. But these people say that ferrets, like other pets, can be trained not to bite. They also point out that there are many more cases of children being bitten seriously by pet dogs than by ferrets. Studies done in the 1980s showed that during one 10-year period, there were 65 reported cases of ferret bites, compared to at least 1 million dog bites. Based on these statistics, dogs are 200 times more likely to bite their human companions than ferrets are.

Finally, several scientific studies have shown that ferrets don't seem to be carriers of the rabies virus. If people are concerned about rabies, however, they can have their pet ferrets vaccinated against the disease, just as they do their pet dogs.

As the public has become more familiar with domesticated ferrets, many of the objections to them have begun to fade away. Organizations of ferret own-

ers, for example, the American Ferret Association, have been working hard in the ferret's defense. In the mid-1990s, only the District of Columbia and two states—California and Hawaii—had laws against owning ferrets. It seems clear that the pet ferret is here to stay.

Choosing a Pet Ferret

People who have decided that a ferret is the pet for them have some choices to make. Where should they get their new pet? Do they want one ferret, or two, or three? Males or females? What color would they prefer?

More and more pet stores now carry ferrets, and many people get their animals there. Others go to local ferret breeders, who often have ads in newspapers or magazines. Ferret babies, called **kits,** are usually sold when they are around 8 to 14 weeks old. Just as in choosing any companion animal, a prospective owner should look for a healthy, active youngster that is used to being around people. Ferrets adopted as adults also make good pets.

Some owners prefer to have two or more pet ferrets so that the animals can keep each other company.

These Siamese ferrets are from the same litter, but ferrets who are not littermates can also get along.

Ferrets are very social animals, and they like being with others of their own kind. For this reason, people often get at least two ferrets. The animals don't have to be from the same **litter** (born at one time from the same mother). Ferrets get along well even if they are not related. It is possible to have just one ferret, but a single animal will need a lot of attention from its human companions.

Pet ferrets are almost always **altered** so that they can't reproduce. (Breeding ferrets is a job best left to experts.) **Neutered** males and **spayed** females make equally good pets. The only important difference between them is size. An adult male ferret, called a **hob,** may be 24 inches (61 cm) long, including the tail, and weigh as much as 5 pounds (2.2 kg). A female, or **jill,** measures at most 18 inches (46 cm) and weighs no more than 3 pounds (1.5 kg). A minor difference is that hobs usually have rounder heads than jills.

Above: *An albino ferret.* Right:
A sable ferret with a silver-mitt,
one of the more unusual
varieties

Like cats, guinea pigs, and other small pets, ferrets come in a variety of colors. The most common color is **sable.** A sable ferret has a dark mask on its face (something like a raccoon's) and a brownish coat with long brownish-black **guard hairs** that stick out from the shorter hairs underneath. This color is most like that of the ferret's wild ancestor, the polecat. Queen Elizabeth's favorite, the red-eyed albino ferret, is still popular. And there are also ferrets with white fur and dark eyes.

By mating specially selected males and females, breeders have developed ferrets with some unusual colors and markings, for example, chocolate, cinnamon, silver-mitt, point, panda, and blaze. As ferrets become more popular, there will probably be even more new colors and markings to choose from.

Living with Ferrets

Having a pet ferret in your home is not quite the same as having a pet dog or cat. Ferrets require some special care, but they also provide some special rewards to their owners.

Most people who have ferrets keep them in indoor cages at least part of the time. These lively little animals can get into trouble if they are always allowed to run free through the house. Ferret cages are usually made of wire and have doors that can be securely fastened. A cage has three separate areas—one for meals, one for sleeping, and one for elimination of wastes. Ferrets are neat, clean animals, and they like to have their "bathrooms" separate from the places that they sleep and eat.

Food dishes for ferrets have to be heavy so they can't be moved around or tipped over. Ferrets are usually given water in bottles that attach to the side of the cage. Like the water containers used for pet rabbits or guinea pigs, the bottles have spouts from which the animals drink. Ferrets need a constant supply of fresh water. They usually eat dry food, either high-quality cat food or special ferret food that is available at many pet stores. Most ferrets also enjoy snacks of raw vegetables and fruits.

Ferrets in their cage with toys, a blanket, and a hammock

Ferrets like to sleep in small, enclosed places. A cage is often equipped with a sleeping box lined with soft, washable material (old cotton T shirts are good). Many ferret owners also provide their pets with cloth hammocks attached to the top of the cages. The animals often take naps two or three at a time in these swinging beds. (Several ferrets can live in the same cage if it is big enough.)

Just like a cat, a ferret uses a plastic box filled with litter for its bathroom. The cage contains a box, and additional ones may be placed in other areas around the house. Ferrets have the instinct always to eliminate their wastes in the same spot. With time and patience, most can be trained to use a litter box. The training is something like that used with pet dogs. Owners make sure that the ferret knows where to go and give it lots of praise when it does the job right.

The cage is the ferret's home, but ferrets don't spend all their time there. Although they may sleep 15 to 20 hours a day, they also need plenty of exercise and play. These things are very important for ferrets. They are active, curious animals and, if kept caged all the time, will get bored, restless, and fat. Most ferret owners let their pets out for at least 1 to 3 hours of exercise and play each day.

After spending most of the day cooped up, ferrets are very happy to get out. To celebrate, they perform what many owners call the ferret "wardance." With back arched, head and tail up, and feet together, the ferret bounces from side to side, making a kind of clucking sound. When new ferret owners see their pet behave in this way, they often think it is having a fit. They soon learn, however, that the dance is just an expression of energy and high spirits.

Ferrets can be trained to walk on a leash.

When they are released from their cages, some ferrets have the run of the whole house. Others are kept in a single room. Wherever ferrets go, they have to be watched carefully. These slim, flexible little animals can get into all kinds of small spaces—and sometimes into a lot of trouble.

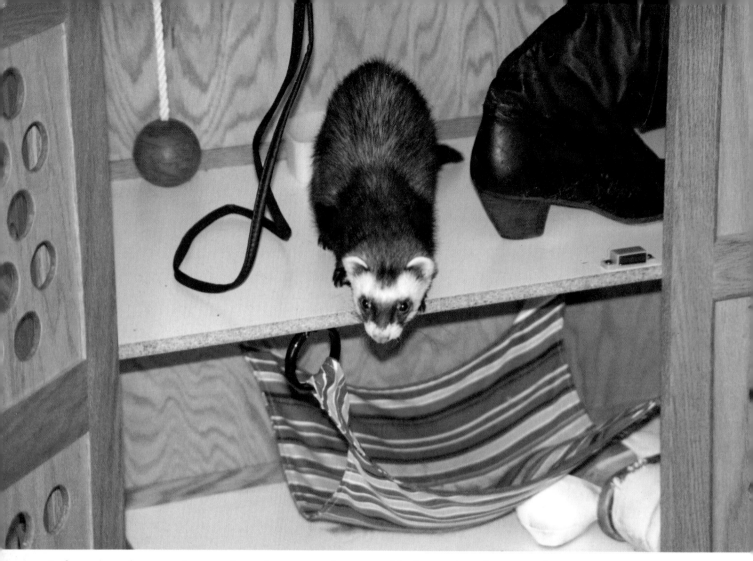

A ferret explores a closet where its owner has provided an extra hammock.

Ferrets love to crawl into and under things. They get into cabinets and dishwashers, inside the stuffing of the sofa, and into heating vents and ducts. They crawl under stoves, refrigerators, rugs, and piles of laundry. Once a ferret finds such a dark, cozy hiding place, it may curl up and go to sleep.

One pet ferret got shut inside a refrigerator when the door was left open, and sleeping was the last thing it wanted to do. Instead, the animal explored the contents of the fridge, opening food containers and throwing eggs around. Luckily, the ferret was found before it was injured by the cold, but its owners had quite a mess to clean up.

Because ferrets can squeeze into very small spaces, it's important to keep an eye on them so that they don't get lost or hurt.

Of course, ferret owners want to prevent their pets from causing this kind of damage or from getting lost. They certainly don't want them to be squashed underfoot or run through the dishwasher. So they keep certain parts of the house off-limits to ferrets and try to "ferret-proof" other areas. They block up all small openings with cardboard, plywood, and tape. They make sure that doors to cabinets and to the outside are shut tight, with no large gaps under them. They watch for suspicious lumps under rugs. They keep the dishwasher, as well as the clothes washer and dryer, closed and check inside before turning them on.

If a ferret does disappear inside the house, people often use a squeaky cat toy to "call" their pet from its hiding place. A ferret will usually respond to this kind of noise and come out to see what is going on. Giving it a favorite treat as a reward will encourage this behavior.

Ferrets can get along with other pets if they are introduced carefully.

Like their wild cousins the otters, ferrets are very playful animals. They can entertain themselves for hours with games. Hide-and-seek is a favorite, of course, and so is tug-of-war (with a washcloth). Ferrets young and old love to run, leap, tumble, wrestle, and chase. They will play with humans, with other ferrets, and even with other pet animals, especially cats.

One game that is popular with ferrets (but not with their owners) is hiding things. The animals love to take small objects and tuck them away in some dark corner. In a home where ferrets live, shoes, socks, car keys, and the TV remote control are always disappearing. Ferrets also hide pieces of food if they have a chance.

Ferrets are very good at entertaining themselves, but most owners also provide their pets with toys. Ferrets like hard balls and other small toys like those used by cats. Their favorite playthings are tubes, pipes, or any other long and narrow thing into which they can crawl. The soft plastic tubing used as the exhaust pipe for a clothes dryer makes a great ferret toy. The animals also enjoy climbing into and out of paper bags or large plastic jugs with holes cut in them.

A ferret having its nails clipped

Ferret Care

Living with a ferret isn't all fun and games. Ferret owners have to provide regular care for their pets.

Ferrets have sharp little claws that need to be clipped from time to time. A ferret's claws are different from the claws of a cat because they cannot be pulled back into the paws. Ferrets don't scratch furniture as cats often do, but their claws can easily get caught in rugs or other material. They can also scratch human skin.

Ferrets don't enjoy having their claws clipped any more than most cats do. It's best to sneak up on them when they are sleeping or keep them occupied with a treat. Cat clippers or human nail clippers can be used for the job.

Another part of ferret care is giving your pet a bath. Like all mustelids, ferrets have scent glands on their rear ends, as well as on the surface of their skin. The musky-smelling fluid produced by these glands gives the ferret's fur an odor that many people find unpleasant. Bathing helps to eliminate this odor.

A ferret that has been spayed or neutered is much less smelly than an un-altered one. This is because the scent glands are most active at the time of mating. (Male ferrets in particular have a very strong odor at this time.) Some people believe that a ferret's odor can also be improved by surgically removing the two anal glands on the animal's rear end. In fact, many young ferrets sold at pet stores have already had this operation, in addition to being altered.

But other experts think that removing the anal glands is an unnecessary step. They claim that a domesticated ferret releases fluid from these glands only when it is afraid or threatened. This does not happen often with a well-cared-for animal. According to this view, having the ferret altered and giving it baths will usually control any odor problem. Good-quality food and clean living conditions also help to keep pet ferrets odor-free.

Ferrets are usually bathed in the kitchen or bathroom sink or in the bathtub. Most don't like water, but a few don't mind getting wet and will even swim if they have a chance. After washing with cat or ferret shampoo and a good rinsing, the ferret must be dried thoroughly with a towel so it doesn't catch cold. Ferrets should be bathed no more than once every other week so that their skin doesn't become too dry.

Ear cleaning is also on the ferret care schedule. Like other pet animals, ferrets can be bothered by ear infections or ear mites. The insides of their small, round ears have to be cleaned with a cotton swab dipped in peroxide or in a special ear cleanser that owners can buy from a veterinarian.

A toy helps make bath time more enjoyable for this young ferret.

Some owners give their ferrets a good-tasting vitamin supplement as a treat.

Regular visits to the vet are necessary for ferrets, as they are for all pets. The animals need yearly shots to prevent canine distemper, a virus that is 100 percent fatal in ferrets. The vet can also give a ferret a shot to prevent rabies.

Taking care of most pet ferrets requires some time and effort but is not difficult. Female ferrets that have not been spayed, however, need special care. If an unaltered female does not mate and produce young regularly, she can become very sick and die. This is due to the domesticated ferret's unusual system of reproduction, which is different from that of cats and dogs.

FERRET
REPRODUCTION

Several times each year, female cats and dogs go through periods during which they are able to mate and produce young. During these periods, the females are said to be in **heat.** (The scientific term for this condition is **estrus.**) A female stays in heat for about 10 to 14 days. If she does not mate, she will go back to her normal life until the next heat period occurs. Male cats and dogs have no periods of heat but can mate anytime they find a willing female.

Ferrets have a different system. Both hobs (males) and jills (females) have special periods during which they can reproduce. These periods are determined by the changing of the seasons, which is why ferrets are known as **seasonal breeders.** In general, ferrets reproduce during spring and summer. As the days become longer in early spring, their bodies get ready for mating and producing young. In the Northern Hemisphere, the ferret breeding season lasts from February or March through August or September.

This jill is ready to mate. She will be put into a cage with a male ferret for breeding.

A mother ferret with her kits

If a hob doesn't find a mate during the breeding season, his health will not be affected. But if a jill doesn't mate after coming into heat, she will very likely die. This is because her body continues to produce reproductive hormones (substances that affect body functions) throughout the long breeding season. These high hormone levels can cause a blood disease called aplastic anemia, which is usually fatal. If the jill doesn't mate and become pregnant, she has to be given shots that will lower the level of hormones in her body.

You can see why having a female ferret that has not been spayed is a big responsibility for a pet owner. Only people who want to breed ferrets usually have unspayed females or unneutered males.

A one-week-old ferret kit

Ferrets kept for breeding often live in outdoor cages or in buildings with a lot of natural light. Since their breeding periods are controlled mainly by changes in the amount of daylight, this is the most natural situation for them. If breeding ferrets live in enclosed areas, artificial light can be used to bring the animals into heat.

When ferrets are ready to mate, the jill is usually put into the hob's cage. The hob is not very gentle with his partner. He grabs her by the back of the neck with his teeth and drags her around before mating. If the mating is successful, the jill will become pregnant. A female ferret carries her young inside her body for about six weeks before giving birth.

A litter of ferret kits, at one week (left) and at three weeks (below)

Most females have 3 to 8 kits at one time, but a litter can be as large as 14 or as small as 1. When a kit is born, it is very tiny, about the size of a person's little finger. Its eyes are closed, and its pink body is covered with fuzzy white hair.

Nourished by their mother's milk, little ferrets grow rapidly. At around four weeks of age, their eyes open. By this time, their adult fur has begun to develop, and colors can be recognized. (Just like a litter of kittens or puppies, a ferret litter can include animals with different colors and markings.) By six weeks, the young ferrets are eating solid food. Until the kits learn how to use their sharp little teeth, their owners often give them dry food soaked in water.

Breeders do all they can to make sure that their ferrets are gentle and friendly.

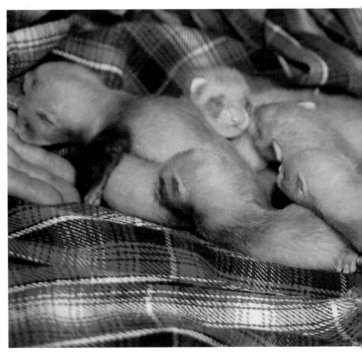

They handle the kits often so that the young animals become used to people. Ferrets raised with affection and care will make good companions when they are adopted by a human family.

THE RETURN OF THE BLACK-FOOTED FERRET

The domesticated ferret lives a pampered life, fed, bathed, and cared for by people. Its wild relative the black-footed ferret almost became extinct because of the actions of humans.

Black-footed ferrets became endangered because of their connection with prairie dogs, small rodents that live on the North American plains. Prairie dogs make up about 90 percent of the black-footed ferret's diet. Prairie-dog burrows provide housing for the little mustelid. When American farmers and ranchers declared war on prairie dogs in the early 1900s, black-footed ferrets became victims in the conflict.

A black-footed ferret emerging from a prairie-dog burrow

Prairie dogs were once a common sight in the American West.

Before that time, ferrets and prairie dogs lived in harmony on the dry, wind-swept plains of the American West. Prairie-dog "towns" with their interconnecting tunnels and burrows covered thousands of acres of land in states such as Wyoming and North and South Dakota. Colonies made up of hundreds of prairie dogs made their homes in these towns. Small numbers of black-footed ferrets also lived there. They built nests in old burrows and caught and killed prairie dogs in the underground tunnels. Coming aboveground mainly at night, the ferrets were seldom seen by humans.

The Native American tribes of the plains knew something about the secretive little animal that shared the prairie dogs' home. Some thought that the black-footed ferret possessed special powers. The Crow made sacred medicine bundles out of the animal's skin. Chiefs of the Cheyennes and Blackfeet wore ferret skins in their headdresses.

41

In the early 1900s, many ranchers and farmers considered prairie-dog burrows a nuisance.

White settlers on the plains did not know much about the black-footed ferret, but they were very familiar with the prairie dog. Ranchers believed that prairie dogs ate precious grass that their cattle needed. Both ranchers and farmers wanted to make use of the land occupied by the extensive prairie-dog towns.

So in the early 1900s, they set out to get rid of the troublesome rodents, with the help of the United States government. They scattered poisoned grain in prairie-dog towns and pumped gas into the burrows. Some towns were destroyed by plows. These programs continued into the 1960s. In some areas, they succeeded in eliminating 99 percent of the prairie-dog population. Prairie dogs were not wiped out, but their numbers were greatly reduced.

As prairie dogs disappeared, so did black-footed ferrets. Without an adequate food supply, many died of starvation, and few young ferrets were born. In 1966, black-footed ferrets were put on the endangered species list. Efforts were made to protect the remaining population, but they failed. By the end of the 1970s, the animals were thought to be extinct.

Then in 1981, a dog on a ranch in Wyoming brought home the body of a long, slim animal that it had killed. It was a black-footed ferret. Searches in the same area turned up a small number of other ferrets. Scientists made studies of the animals and took a few into captivity. But the captive ferrets died of canine distemper, and the same disease began to attack the wild population. Researchers were faced with a difficult decision. What should they do to make sure that the few remaining black-footed ferrets in the wild survived?

A black-footed ferret with a prairie dog it has killed.

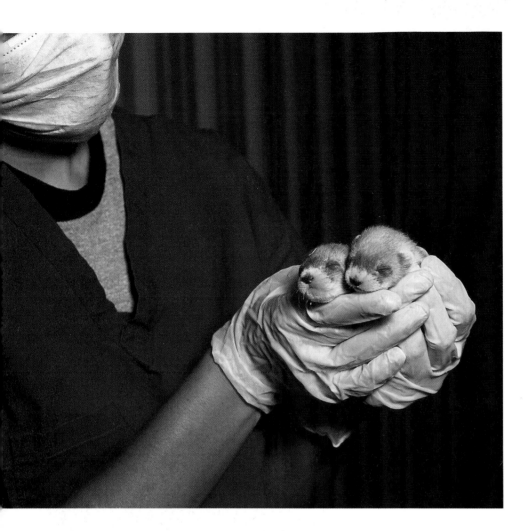

A researcher examines some black-footed ferret kits that were born in captivity.

Finally, in 1985 the Wyoming Game and Fish Department decided to capture all the black-footed ferrets that they could find. By taking the animals into captivity, wildlife officials hoped to protect them and also to find ways to increase the population through breeding. It was a daring move, and not all wildlife researchers thought that it was a wise one. But despite many ups and downs, the plan to save the black-footed ferret seems to have been a success.

In 1986, 18 black-footed ferrets were taken into captivity. By 1991, the number of captive ferrets had increased to over 200, thanks to successful breeding programs. In that year, Wyoming officials began releasing a few of the animals back into the wild. Raised in captivity, the released ferrets were not very good at avoiding predators. Many were killed by coyotes, but a few survived.

Life for the black-footed ferret (left) is not as easy as for its pampered cousin the domesticated ferret (below).

Since the early 1990s, the captive population of black-footed ferrets has grown steadily, reaching about 400 in 1995. More animals have been released, after first going through a "training" period in fenced-in prairie-dog towns at research centers. Here ferrets can practice their hunting skills, safe from attack by other animals. When they are released, some are still killed by predators, but others survive and produce young.

Once again, black-footed ferrets are living on the North American plains. Whether they continue to survive will largely depend on the actions of people. Like the domesticated ferret, the black-footed ferret now has close connections with the world of humans. If we treat this wild animal with some of the same respect and concern that we give to our pet ferrets, it may have a good chance for life.

GLOSSARY

albinos: animals lacking the pigments that produce color in fur, eyes, and other body parts. Albinos have white fur; their eyes appear red because of blood vessels close to the surface.

altered: having reproductive organs removed so that an animal cannot have young

anal glands: scent glands on a mustelid's rear end used to discharge fluids in self-defense

carnivores: animals that eat meat

chromosomes: the individual units of genetic material contained in the body's cells

estrus: the period during which a female animal is able to reproduce. Also called *heat.*

ferreting: using domesticated ferrets to hunt rabbits or other small animals

guard hairs: long, stiff hairs that stick out from the under layer of an animal's fur

heat: the period during which a female animal is able to reproduce

hob: a male ferret

jill: a female ferret

kits: baby ferrets

litter: a group of young animals born at the same time to one mother

mustelids: animals that belong to the scientific family Mustelidae. Minks, otters, skunks, badgers, polecats, and domesticated ferrets are all mustelids.

neutered: having male reproductive organs removed

sable: the most common coloring of a domesticated ferret. A sable ferret has brownish fur and a dark mask on its face.

scent glands: structures in an animal's body that produce smelly substances used in communication or self-defense

seasonal breeders: animals whose breeding periods are controlled by the changing of the seasons

spayed: having female reproductive organs removed

INDEX

ABOUT THE AUTHOR

Sylvia A. Johnson has had a long and productive career as an editor and writer of books for young people. She has worked on publications about such diverse subjects as a beekeeper and his bees, life in a wolf pack, and just what goes on inside a fertilized chicken egg.

Although the majority of Ms. Johnson's books are in the area of the social and natural sciences, her own academic background is in English and literature. She received a B.A. in English from Marian College in Indiana and an M.A. in the same subject at the University of Illinois. In her years as an editor and writer, Ms. Johnson has collaborated with writers in the fields of archaeology, botany, behavioral biology, and many other fascinating subjects. Doing research for her own books, she has explored the tallgrass prairie, observed surgery on injured raptors, and donned a bee suit and veiled hat to get a closeup look at a beekeeper at work.

Sylvia A. Johnson makes her home in Minneapolis, where she lives in a gray-shingled house with Smokey, a small but dignified gray-striped cat.